FINDING GOD IN THE BIBLE

FINDING GOD *IN THE* *BIBLE*

A BEGINNER'S

GUIDE TO

KNOWING

GOD | KEN WILSON

MOODY PUBLISHERS
CHICAGO

Scripture taken from the *Holy Bible, New International Version*®. NIV®. Copyright © 1973, 1978, 1984 by International Bible Society. Used by permission of Zondervan Publishing House. All rights reserved.

Library of Congress Cataloging-in-Publication Data

Wilson, Ken (Ken Edgar), 1957-
  Finding God in the Bible: a beginner's guide to knowing God / Ken Wilson.
    p.cm.
    Includes bibliographical references.
  ISBN-13: 978-0-8024-1442-7
  1. Salvation 2. Christian Life. I. Title.
  BT751.3.W55 2005
  248.4–dc22

ISBN: 0-8024-1442-7
ISBN-13: 978-0-8024-1442-7

1 3 5 7 9 10 8 6 4 2

Printed in the United States of America

This Booklet Belongs to

_____

I Began it On

_____

To
Mom and Dad,
whose love and faithfulness
made it easier for me to trust
a loving and faithful God

CONTENTS

Introduction

Finding God in the Bible provides a starting place for getting to know God. It is a study and discussion guide based upon what the Bible says about beginning a close, personal relationship with your Creator.

Each of us faces countless choices and decisions—from the daily matters of what clothes to put on in the morning and what food to prepare for dinner, to the more important decisions of whom to marry and what career to embark upon. No decision that you will ever make, however, will be more important or will have a more lasting impact than what you choose to do with Jesus Christ.

Before you begin this booklet, take a few moments to respond to the following two questions. Write down your answers as honestly as possible.

What do you think it means to be a Christian?

_____

_____

How would you respond if God were to ask you today, "Why should I let you into My heaven?"

_____

_____

The first question will evoke various answers from different people. The purpose of this booklet, however, is to help you discover what God has to say about what it means to be a Christian. After all, being God, what He says is what truly counts!

If you had trouble answering the second question, then this booklet is certainly for you. If your answer referred to your personal merit, your religious credentials, or your good lifestyle, you may be in for a surprise as you find out more about what God says in His Word.

Finding God in the Bible will help you discover the wonderful plan God has revealed to us in the Bible. God desires for you to *know,* with assurance, that your future and eternal home will be with Him in a perfect place.

As you begin your journey through God's Word, you may wish to pause for a few moments to tell God what's on your mind and heart. Your prayer may sound something like this:

> *God, I admit that I don't know You very well (and I'm not even sure if I know You at all). I want to know You though, and I want to learn how You can bring meaning and purpose and direction to my life, right here and now. I ask that as I read this booklet, You will reveal Yourself to me. I pray that You will allow me to know You in a very real and profound way. And finally, God, I ask that You'll supply me with the faith and the conviction to follow You and to act on the truth that You reveal to me. Thank You for hearing my prayer, and I look forward to receiving Your answer. Amen.*

How to Use this Booklet

This booklet was written to serve as a tool in helping you uncover the best news mankind has ever known.

This is what you will find in each chapter:

Introduction page—includes a brief introduction and a simple drawing (beginning in chapter 2) that illustrates the chapter's message. Each drawing is built upon in the subsequent chapters. (These sketches are adapted from a tract by The Navigators called *Bridge to Life.*[1] For information about obtaining copies of this tract, see page 89.)

Up Close and Personal—provides two real-life portraits of people for whom the chapter's message has been especially significant, the first presenting portions of other people's spiritual pilgrimages and the second revealing parts of my own.

Getting Started—offers you a few thought-provoking questions to ponder as you begin each chapter.

Digging Deeper—provides the meat of the chapter, guiding you to central portions of the Bible.

Illustration—presents a simple story to enhance your understanding of the chapter.

Food for Thought—provides two quotes to challenge you, dealing with the chapter's message, by Christian leaders and influential personalities from both today and centuries past.

Memory Verse—presents one Bible passage to memorize that is central to the surrounding teaching.

Mileposts—offers you a place to record some of the things that you have learned.

Moving On—wraps up the chapter and introduces the next chapter.

Here are some tips to help you make the most of this booklet:

What You'll Need

The only things you will need are a pen or pencil, a Bible, and an open heart. You'll benefit the most if you are honest with yourself and God.

Set Your Own Pace

This booklet is designed to be adaptable to your schedule. I recommend you set aside some time on either a daily, weekly, or biweekly basis. Weekly sessions may offer the best solution for providing continuity within busy schedules. (The last session, *After Accepting Christ,* is longer than the other chapters and may require more time.) Whatever time frame works best for you, you'll be most successful if you commit to it and complete the whole booklet.

Get Together in a Small Group

Finding God in the Bible can be used in a variety of settings. One of the best is within a small group of neighbors, co-workers, or family members. A small group can provide encouragement, accountability, and intimacy. It can be a good environment for care and nurture, where we can let our masks down and be real. (For additional information, see "Using this Booklet in a Small Group" on page 77.)

Get Together with a Friend

This booklet may also be studied one-on-one with a friend. Like a small group, this can also provide accountability, mentoring, and friendship. If one of you is seeking to explore what a relationship with Christ is about, I recommend pairing up with someone who has been consistently nurturing their relationship with Him for a while. (For additional information, see "Using this Booklet with a Friend" on page 81.)

Go Ahead and Write

This booklet was written to be written in! Throughout the booklet, questions are presented with space for you to record your responses. Many of the questions are about you—there is no right or wrong answer as long as you are honest! Other questions deal with passages of the Bible—for those, simply write your answers, as best you can, based on the particular Bible passage that you read. In *Mileposts,* record some of the things that you sense God may be teaching you. Throughout the booklet, record questions, insights, struggles, conclusions, and anything else you want to write. These notes may be helpful to you later on.

Look Up the Verses

Please look up the Bible passages. This booklet offers little or no value without the accompanying Bible verses. Neglecting to look them up will remove this booklet's source of power and truth, much like trying to drive a car with no engine in it.

Use a Modern Translation

Although the Bible can be a little intimidating and sometimes difficult to understand, it doesn't have to be that way. In the past several decades, the Bible has been translated into several modern English versions. These new translations are careful to retain the accuracy of the original text while, at the same time, presenting it in a language that we use and understand today. These modern English translations include (but are not exclusive to) the New International Version (NIV), the Revised Standard Version (RSV), the New American Standard Version (NASB), the New King James Version (NKJV), and the New Living Translation (NLT). Any of these modern English translations will help you get the most from your study of this booklet and the Bible. (The memory verses in this booklet are presented in the New International Version.)

How to Use the Bible

The Bible is presented in books, chapters, and verses to make it simpler to use and to reference. Bible references are written in a manner that presents the book, the chapter, and then the verse. For example, John 3:16 means that you are to look up the book of John, the 3rd chapter and the 16th verse. If you need help, use the table of contents in the front of your Bible to assist you.

Read the Whole Story

Although you will be looking up individual verses and passages in the Bible to respond to the questions in this booklet, these verses and passages were not originally written to stand alone. They were written in a unique context and setting. Each verse of the Bible complements and sheds light on our understanding of every other verse. To learn the most from a particular passage, you may wish to read a few verses before and a few verses after the specified passage to better understand its context.

You are now ready to embark upon a great adventure leading you to a matchless treasure. Enjoy your journey as you discover what the Bible says about beginning a personal relationship with your Creator and getting to know the living God.

❶ *God's Plan*
AN ABUNDANT LIFE

God purposely created you, and He loves you more than you can fathom. He desires for you to experience joy and peace, and He has a plan for your life. God longs for you to know Him personally and intimately and offers you eternal life with meaning and fullness, beginning here on earth and reaching permanent perfection in heaven.

Up Close and Personal

|AURA is a delightful young woman with a caring nature and a great big heart. Her life, however, has been filled with difficult experiences. As a child, she was abandoned by her father, berated or ignored by her mother, and abused by a relative. As an adult, circumstances have repeatedly turned against her, and her self-esteem has taken a beating. During a period of utter despair, she considered taking her own life. Fortunately, in her search for meaning, she found that God loves her deeply. Even though others had not valued her in the past, Laura's point of view changed as she discovered that the Creator of the universe does not make junk—God uniquely created her to have her specific, loving disposition. While she still faces struggles and problems, they no longer dominate her life. God's love has brought her a noticeable peace, allowing her to love others and Him in return.

I was fortunate to be raised in a loving family. I have many wonderful memories from my childhood. However, I also struggled with a speech impediment. As the teasing of junior high classmates ripped into my sensitive nature, a strong shield prevented those destructive darts from wounding my self-esteem. That shield was an abiding assurance that the God who created me also loves me with a deeper love than my limited mind could grasp. My self-worth was not derived from what classmates said or how well I performed—it was rooted in God's matchless love for me. As the years passed, these childhood convictions were further tested by a broken engagement, a stillborn daughter, and two miscarriages. Through the tears and sorrows of those experiences came a priceless treasure—a deeper intimacy with God than ever before. I gained an even deeper conviction that the God who made me and loves me also knows what is best for me and can be trusted to ultimately take care of all things, regardless of my circumstances.

Getting Started

1. What are some of the things that are good and very special about you? (Don't be humble!)

   _____

   _____

   _____

   _____

2. What do you consider to be the major goals or purposes in your life?

   _____

   _____

   _____

   _____

   _____

   _____

3. What are some of the first things that come to mind when you think of God?

   _____

   _____

   _____

   _____

Digging Deeper

1. Read John 3:16 in your Bible. According to this verse, whom does God love?

   _____

   Does that include you?

   _____

   What did His love cause Him to do?

   _____

2. Based on John 10:10, what kind of life does God desire for you?

   _____

   What do you think Jesus meant by a full and abundant life?

   _____

3. According to Psalm 139:13–16, who created you?

   _____

   What does this passage say about the care with which He made you?

   _____

4. One of the first goals of this booklet is to shed light on the character of God. While God is far too wonderful and awesome for our limited minds

to fully comprehend, we can be thankful that He has chosen to reveal a great deal about Himself to us through the Bible.

For each of the Bible verses listed in the table below, write a characteristic of God that is described by the passage.

Bible Verses	Characteristics
Psalm 90:2	
Romans 16:27	
1 Corinthians 1:9	
Ephesians 1:18–19	
2 Thessalonians 1:6	
1 Peter 1:15–16	
1 John 4:8, 16	

5. Do you believe God loves you? Why?

Illustration

We went out one evening and left our children under the care of a baby sitter. When we returned about midnight, the girl was greatly concerned because our oldest child had been crying for about four hours. Nothing that the baby sitter could do would comfort her.

I went to the child's room and found her flushed and sobbing, her face red with weeping. When I picked her up, she threw her arms around my neck and sobbed, "Daddy, say it isn't true. You do love me." I replied that of course I loved her, and then the child said, "She said that if I was bad you wouldn't love me, and I know that I've been bad, so maybe you do not love me."

I pressed her to me and said, "My dear child, I always love you. When you are good I love you with a love that makes me glad; when you are bad I love you with a love that makes me sad. But I love you, good or bad. I am always your daddy."

The child was already more calm, and the dawn of a smile came to her face. I kissed her and told her that a good daddy would love like God the Father loves His Son Jesus and the rest of His children. His love is always with them. She smiled and soon drifted off to sleep.[2]

Food for Thought

"You have made us for Yourself, O God, and our hearts are restless until they find their rest in You."[3]
Augustine

"There is a God-shaped vacuum in the heart of every man which only God can fill through His Son, Jesus Christ."
Blaise Pascal

Memory Verse

"For God so loved the world that he gave his one and only Son, that whoever believes in him shall not perish but have eternal life."—John 3:16

Mileposts

What are some of the things that God has taught you from your study of this chapter?

Moving On

Did you know that God loves *you?*

God loves you passionately. God loves you completely. He loves you as though you were the only person in the whole world to love. Just as the father in our story loved his child unconditionally, so God loves and treasures you. You are His precious creation. People are worth more to Him than anything else under the heavens.

There is nothing you can do to make God love you more, or love you less. You are the apple of His eye, the delight of His heart, His beloved creation. He is thinking of you every passing moment, and just the thought of you brings a smile to His face. He loves you even before you love Him![4]

God purposely chose to create you. You are here because He deliberately made you and wants you to be here. He wants a personal relationship with you and desires for you to have peace and joy, some of which you will experience here on earth, though it is available without measure in heaven.

Since God planned for us to have peace and abundant life beginning right now, why are most people not experiencing this? The next chapter deals with humanity's problem. Just as children disobey their parents, we have made decisions that are contrary to God's good desires for us.

❷ *Our Problem*
SIN AND SEPARATION

From the beginning, we have broken God's laws and failed to live up to His standards. We have chosen to disobey Him and go our own ways. We still choose to disobey, and the Bible calls this sin. We are sinful in our very nature and in the way we live. God, on the other hand, is both holy (that is, absolutely pure) and just (that is, a good judge). Our sinful nature separates us from God, both in this life and throughout eternity. We stand morally bankrupt and spiritually helpless before God.

Us

God

God loves you, He wants a personal relationship with you, and He offers you an abundant life.

We are all sinful, and this results in separation from God.

Up Close and Personal

JEFF had lived through many torturous years that included an affair in his marriage, job dismissals, and months in the jungles of Vietnam. His career, marriage, and family were in turmoil. Eventually, his consuming stresses caused a bleeding ulcer that almost claimed his life. During this same time, Jeff's friend Fred was living a comfortable life and was considered by many to be an ideal citizen (Fred had offered to donate his bone marrow to save the life of a stranger). Fred was a devoted friend to many, characterized by inner goodness plus a handsome exterior. Yet both Jeff and Fred shared several common characteristics. Both felt an inner longing to be right with God, both tried to fill that need on their own merit, and both felt a desperate helplessness to please God on their own. And, ultimately, both came face-to-face with their need for a Savior to rescue them from themselves and from sin's penalty.

I was a fourth-grade hotshot when I learned that I couldn't live a perfect life. As class president (which meant absolutely nothing in terms of responsibility and power) and a straight-A student, my head began to swell. One morning, trying to justify my puffed-up pride, I decided that I'd be perfect in every way for an entire day. I made it little more than an hour before I became conscious of a thought or behavior that was less than godly. So I decided to repeat my experiment the next morning. And then the next, and the next. It took me but a week to realize that the nine-year-old boy staring back at me in the mirror was powerless to live a life wholly pleasing to God. For the first time, I saw myself for who I really am, someone who misses the mark of God's perfect standard and is powerless to cleanse his own heart.

Getting Started

1. If you could change anything about your character or the way you live, what would you change?

_____

_____

_____

2. Place an "X" where you feel you belong on the following "goodness scale"[5]:

Perfect, just like God

As low as low can be

3. Take a moment or two to think of instances when you know you've done wrong and have fallen short of how God would want you to live. Without writing any words, make a dot in the following box for each instance you can think of.[6]

Digging Deeper

1. According to the following passages, what does God say about us and sin?

   Psalm 14:3

   _____

   Isaiah 64:6

   _____

   Romans 3:23

   _____

2. Do you think this applies to your life?   ❏ **Yes**   ❏ **No**

3. Based upon the following verses, list some characteristics associated with sin:

Bible Verses	Sin Characteristics
Psalm 51:5	
Jeremiah 17:9	
James 2:10	

4. According to the Bible, what are the results or consequences of our sinful nature?

   Isaiah 59:1–2

   _____

   2 Thessalonians 1:8–9

   _____

   Romans 6:23

   _____

5. In your own words, what do you think the following key words mean, as used in Romans 6:23?

   wages

   _____

   sin

   _____

   death

   _____

Illustration

Three people stood at the end of a dock along the California coast, determined to swim across the Pacific Ocean to the paradise of the Hawaiian Islands. The first swimmer had religiously gone to the pool almost every Sunday of his life. He felt he had made a decent effort at learning how to swim well, at least as much as could be expected, and he was probably as good as or better than most. Surely, he thought, this would get him across the ocean to paradise. However, as he jumped off the dock and began to swim, he made it only a few miles before he began to sink.

The second swimmer not only went to the pool each Sunday, but also began each day with a mile swim and ended it with another mile swim. She held countless positions at the swim club, she tirelessly studied the physiology and psychology of swimming, and she selflessly helped others in their pursuit of swimming excellence. Her dedication to swimming and her hard work earned her the respect of her swimming peers around the world. As she dove into the water and began her long journey, her powerful and graceful strokes carried her over twenty miles through the mounting waves and mighty currents of the Pacific Ocean. However, eventually she could make it no longer and drowned.

Finally, the third swimmer readied himself for the long swim. He was undoubtedly the greatest swimmer the world had ever known, sweeping eight gold medals for swimming in each of the past four Olympic Games. Not only had he broken every record the swimming world had to offer, but he had shattered them, leaving his peers with virtually no hope of ever matching his swimming excellence. He, too, dove into the waters and swam off into the horizon as well-wishing onlookers lined the coast as far as the eye could see. He was truly the best mankind had to offer, and he had no equal in his surpassing greatness. As nightfall came, he had passed the locations where each of the first two swimmers had drowned, and his strokes were still powerful and effective. Eventually, however, his greatest efforts also fell short, and he, too, sank to the bottom of the ocean.

A pilot flying overhead observed that he had swum over 250 miles toward his desired destination before going under, a feat unmatched in human history. However, the pilot also noted that the champion swimmer's best efforts got him just over one-tenth of the way to paradise.[7]

Food for Thought

"Man seeks to excuse himself of sin, but God seeks to convict him of it and to save him from it. Sin incurs the penalty of death, and no man has the ability in himself to save himself from sin's penalty or to cleanse his own heart of its corruption."[8]

Billy Graham

"Sin is the only thing that God abhors. It brought Christ to the cross, it damns souls, it shuts heaven, it laid the foundation of hell."

Thomas Brooks

Memory Verse

"For the wages of sin is death, but the gift of God is eternal life in Christ Jesus our Lord."—Romans 6:23

Mileposts

What are some of the things that God has taught you from your study of this chapter?

Moving On

A deadly problem has invaded planet earth, and the Bible says that every human is inflicted with it.

If you placed your "X" even a fraction of an inch from the top of the "goodness scale" or if you placed even one dot in the box, then you test positive and you, too, are inflicted. The Bible identifies this deadly problem with a name: sin. The Bible also reveals the consequences of our sin: eternal separation from God.

"All God expects of me is a decent effort," we often think, "and if I live a life free of big sins like murder, then I must be doing okay. At least I'm not as bad as (so-and-so)!"

However, in reality, God's benchmark for morality is His perfect purity and holiness. Whether in our thoughts or in our actions, whether in things we've done or in things we haven't done, our lives have consistently fallen short of His goodness. Just as the swimmers' best efforts were pitifully insufficient, so are ours.

With each dot in the box, we are essentially telling God, "I know what You want, but too bad! I'm doing it my way!" And whether you placed your "X" near the bottom of the "goodness scale" or just a bit below the top, you have fallen short of God's perfect standard.

A pure God and impure people are simply not compatible. Our sin ultimately leads to death, both physical and spiritual. It separates us from God, both in this life and throughout eternity. And because God is holy and just, He cannot compromise His perfect standards.

If we want God to meet us on the grounds of our own merit, we stand condemned and are as good as dead. We are incapable of rescuing ourselves from the eternal consequences of our sin.

Like the drowning swimmers, we need someone to make up the difference between our best efforts and God's perfect standard. Who can make up this difference? Who can take the hit for our sin? How can God's justice that demands a penalty of eternal separation from a perfect God, and His love that longs for an eternal relationship of love and intimacy with us both be perfectly satisfied? The next chapter deals with God's remedy. It is the reason the message in this booklet is known as the gospel, which means "good news"!

God's Remedy
THE CROSS OF CHRIST

Jesus Christ is God, who also became man. He is the only solution to our problem of sin and separation from God. When Jesus died on the cross, He paid the penalty that we owe for our sin. He rose from the grave, defeating the power of death, as we also will rise again after death to eternal life if we accept Jesus' payment for our sins. He died as our substitute and bridged the gap between us and God. Christ offers us His forgiveness as a free gift. His death and resurrection make a new, eternal (everlasting) life possible.

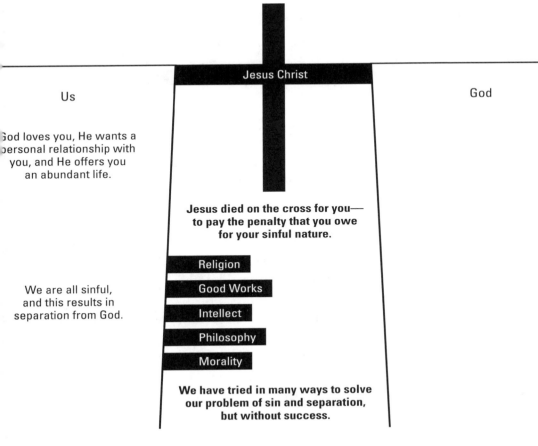

Jesus Christ

Us

God

God loves you, He wants a personal relationship with you, and He offers you an abundant life.

Jesus died on the cross for you—
to pay the penalty that you owe
for your sinful nature.

Religion

Good Works

Intellect

Philosophy

Morality

We are all sinful, and this results in separation from God.

We have tried in many ways to solve
our problem of sin and separation,
but without success.

Up Close and Personal

KAREN *is no stranger to death. During Karen's young-adult years, her mother died of cancer, and this disease claimed her father's life a short time later. Her brother-in-law committed suicide, and her younger brother, who was also one of her best friends, died in a motorcycle accident. One thing after another, including difficult issues with her son, led Karen's husband to our doorstep in tears. Through this string of events, Karen and her husband found themselves sitting in our living room amongst a small group of nine couples while a friend explained the message of this chapter. As we listened to the illustration presented at the end of this chapter, tears welled up in Karen's eyes. She began to comprehend, for the first time, the incredible price her Creator had paid for her, giving up His own Son out of His love for her. Karen has not yet committed her life to the Lord, but God is gently working in her heart and drawing her closer to Himself.*

During the years of my youth, my personal theology was very simple—God loves me, and if I'm good enough, hopefully it'll get me into heaven. (Being good, of course, was relative to the bell curve of everyone else. Or, at least, it meant that the good stuff I did outweighed the bad stuff.) Then, when my family moved and I began tenth grade, Jay Davis entered my life and challenged my beliefs at their very core. Among other things, Jay told me that my sinful nature separates me from God, that I can't be good enough to make it into heaven, and that this is the reason Jesus died in my place. He also told me that I can know God personally and intimately, that Jesus claims to be the only way, and that faith is the key to the whole thing. Being a red-blooded adolescent, I wasn't about to let anyone else tell me what to believe. The last thing I wanted was to believe something that was not true or was merely a crutch. I did the only thing I could—I called Jay a religious fanatic and emphatically told him to "knock it off!"

Getting Started

1. Almost everyone wants to go to heaven. If you were asked to submit an application for admittance into heaven, what would you state as your qualifications?

> **Application for Admittance into Heaven**
>
> *What are your qualifications for admittance into heaven?*

2. Do you think the qualifications that you presented above will be sufficient?   ❑ **Yes**   ❑ **No**   ❑ **I hope so**   ❑ **I don't know**

3. What is the greatest gift that you ever received? What made it so special?

   _____

   _____

4. If a friend asked you to describe Jesus using one or two sentences, how would you respond?

   _____

   _____

   _____

   _____

   _____

Digging Deeper

1. Look up the word "mediator" in the dictionary. Write its meaning in your own words.

   _____

   _____

   _____

   According to 1 Timothy 2:5–6, who is in need of a mediator?

   _____

   _____

   How many mediators are there between God and people?

   _____

   _____

   Who is our mediator?

   _____

   _____

2.

Bible Verses	What did Jesus do to pay the penalty for our sin?	Why did He do this?
Romans 5:6–8		
1 Peter 2:24		
1 Peter 3:18		

3. Write the following passages in your own words.

John 14:6

_____

_____

_____

_____

_____

_____

Acts 4:12

_____

_____

_____

_____

_____

_____

John 3:16–18, 36

_____

_____

_____

_____

_____

_____

4. According to the passages on the previous page, are there any other ways, other than through Jesus, by which we can be saved? Why or why not? *(Being "saved" is a word used to describe our being rescued from the eternal consequences of our sin.)*

_____

_____

_____

_____

_____

_____

_____

_____

_____

_____

_____

5.

Bible Verses	What role does faith play in our salvation?	What role does good works play in our salvation?
Romans 3:20–24, 27–28		
Galatians 2:16		
Ephesians 2:8–9		

(God's grace simply means God's favor toward us though we don't deserve it, or "God's riches at Christ's expense.")

6. Do you think we can take any credit for our salvation? Why or why not?

_____

_____

_____

_____

_____

_____

7. Take a look at what you wrote on page 35 in your application for admittance into heaven. According to the Bible passages we just read, do you think this will be sufficient? Why or why not?

_____

_____

_____

_____

_____

_____

Illustration

A young man and his son decided to spend the day together, as they typically did each Saturday. As they set out early in the morning, they hadn't yet decided if they would hike through the woods, go to the ball game, or try to catch some trout together. It went without saying that regardless of whatever decision they made, their greatest delight would be in simply being together for the day.

Their first stop was the local train station where the father was the operator of the nearby drawbridge. As the father and son jumped out of the car, the son made his way up onto his daddy's shoulders and they walked along the tracks a few hundred yards to the drawbridge station. As they walked along, the two laughed and carried on, basking in the joy of one another's company. As the son climbed down from his daddy's shoulders, the father quickly immersed himself in his railroad work so that he could then get on with the real order of business—a day of frolicking and fun with his cherished son.

Suddenly, a train whistle broke through the silence. Alarmed by the fact that a train was quickly approaching, the father was immediately overcome by two observations—that the drawbridge was not in position for a train to pass and that his son had wandered off and was nowhere to be found. As he searched for his son, a terrified look engulfed the father's face—his son was playing in the gears of the drawbridge and would be crushed to death if the bridge was lowered into position for the train to pass. Realizing that he had no time to remove his son from the gears and that the lives of several hundred train passengers were at stake, the father was overcome with grief at his impending decision.

After a few moments of lonely anguish, the father slowly but deliberately pulled the lever, turning the gears of the drawbridge and lowering it into position for the train to safely pass to the other side. He then turned his face away so as not to look upon the agonizing death of his beloved son.

However, when he finally did turn to look at the drawbridge, he noticed something about the passengers on the train as it traveled off into the horizon. They were laughing among themselves and having a grand old time, unaware of the price that had just been paid for their very lives and ungrateful for the father's sacrifice of his dear son. The father slowly and quietly walked away, tears streaming from his eyes, sorrow written on every crease in his face.[9]

Food for Thought

"A man may go to heaven without health, without riches, without honors, without learning, without friends, but he can never go there without Christ."
John Dyer

"If there be ground for you to trust in your own righteousness, then all that Christ did to purchase salvation, and all that God did to prepare the way for it, is in vain."
Jonathan Edwards

Memory Verse

"For it is by grace you have been saved, through faith—and this not from yourselves, it is the gift of God—not by works, so that no one can boast."—Ephesians 2:8–9

Mileposts

What are some of the things that God has taught you from your study of this chapter?

Moving On

Last chapter, we learned that all of us fall short of God's benchmark of perfect purity and holiness. None of us can place our "X" at the very top of the "goodness scale."

Now look back at the qualifications you presented in your application for admittance into heaven. Do they focus on your best attempts at living a good life, your better-than-average lifestyle, or your religious credentials?

If so, then you are depending on the wrong thing! Your best attempts, your good life, your moral lifestyle, and your religious credentials *all fall hopelessly short of God's perfection and are completely powerless to make you right with God!*

You, my friend, stand in need of a Savior!

And this is where Jesus magnificently enters the picture!

The wonderful news of the Bible is that Jesus did for us what we could never do for ourselves. He paid the full penalty for our sins when He died on the cross. Jesus alone is holy and righteous enough to take the hit for us, and because of His passionate, complete love for us, He willingly did so.

Jesus shed His blood for our sins so that we wouldn't have to experience spiritual death and eternal separation from God. Jesus voluntarily paid for our sin by dying on the cross as our substitute. We are the reason that He gave His life. Jesus died to pay the price for you; He ransomed you with His blood.

Jesus' death on the cross was not only to secure your entrance into heaven. It was also to secure for you an abundant and eternal life that begins here on earth, characterized by forgiveness, purpose, peace, and joy. And God's motive was pure and simple—a deep, incomprehensible love for you and me. Just as the father in our story willingly sacrificed his dearly beloved son, so God willingly gave His only Son in your place, for *you.*

The Bible makes it clear that Jesus' death alone has the power to save us. It says that only the cross and blood of Christ can make us clean before God. Just as the swimmers in the last chapter illustrate, our own efforts and our good works always fall short, and we cannot earn our way to heaven.

Our salvation (being saved from both the enslaving power and the eternal consequences of our sin) is a free gift. And it is available for everyone to receive. How does what Jesus did become effective in our own lives? The next chapter deals with the necessity of our response to God's free offer of salvation. It also tells us how we can enter into a personal relationship with our Creator.

❹ *Our Response*
RECEIVE CHRIST

Even though Jesus died for everyone, we must personally respond to His death on our behalf. We must individually receive Him into our lives, and we must trust Him to do what He has promised—forgive our sins and give us eternal life with Him.

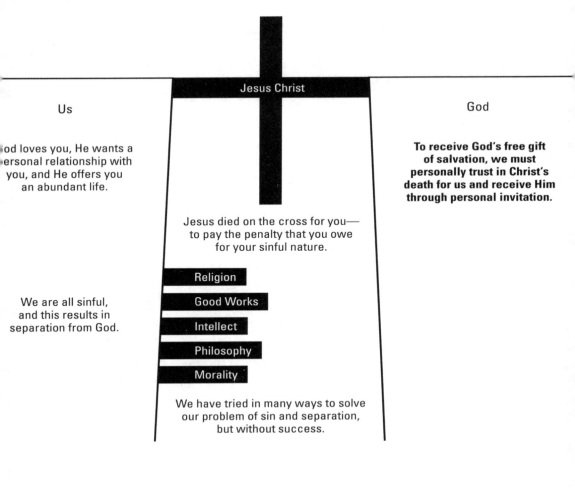

Us

God

Jesus Christ

God loves you, He wants a personal relationship with you, and He offers you an abundant life.

To receive God's free gift of salvation, we must personally trust in Christ's death for us and receive Him through personal invitation.

Jesus died on the cross for you— to pay the penalty that you owe for your sinful nature.

Religion

Good Works

Intellect

Philosophy

Morality

We are all sinful, and this results in separation from God.

We have tried in many ways to solve our problem of sin and separation, but without success.

Up Close and Personal

JACK and I were college roommates for three years at Cornell. I quickly admired that he cared about the things that matter most and that he was going to be himself regardless of what others thought. As our friendship grew, we challenged each other in many areas, including our sexual standards. He couldn't comprehend why anyone would choose to wait and save sex for marriage. We also challenged each other's spiritual convictions—he had been raised with very few, but he was soon reading the entire New Testament to find out about Jesus for himself. As he read, he became convinced that the Jesus of the Bible is the true God, and he felt compelled to get to know Him. Throughout the fall of our senior year, he wrestled with a life-changing decision. If he was going to commit his life to Jesus, he would also have to live his life God's way, including his sex life. Sometime that fall, Jack invited the Lord to come into his life. Trusting that God's ways are best, he let Him be the Ruler of his life. Jack became a new person that day. And we're both glad he did.

My sixteenth year was pivotal for me. As I wrestled with all that Jay was teaching me, my mind couldn't explain away the historical evidence for Jesus' resurrection nor could it reason away the many prophecies recorded in the Old Testament that Jesus fulfilled. Even more significant, my heart began to see that Jesus transforms lives, and my many friends who had a relationship with Him were living proof. While I desired the peace and hope that they had, I also feared the unknown of giving my life to a God I can not physically see. Finally, one summer night after my sophomore year, I came to the point of surrender—I accepted Christ into my life and decided to trust Him as my Savior. There were no fireworks or dramatic revelations, and to be truthful, I wanted to get Jay off my back. But my commitment was also very genuine, and God gently invaded and gloriously transformed my life—and He continues to do so today, twenty-five years later.

Getting Started

1. In the illustration on page 47, which side of the gap do you think you're on right now? Write your name there.

_____

_____

2. What are you depending on to make you acceptable to God?

_____

_____

3. If your earthly life were to end today, do you know for certain where you would spend eternity? If not, do you want to know for sure?

_____

_____

4. Can you point to a time in your life (either a specific day or a period of time) when you placed your trust in Jesus for your salvation and you invited Him into your life? If so, describe what happened in your life because of that decision.

_____

_____

_____

_____

_____

_____

Digging Deeper

1. Before we go any further, let's take a closer look at some vivid portraits of Jesus presented in both the Old Testament and the New Testament. The Old Testament continually proclaims "the Savior is coming!" The prophet Isaiah foretold the coming of Jesus in detail more than six hundred years before He was even born. What description does the prophet provide of Jesus in Isaiah 53:1–8?

_____

_____

_____

_____

_____

2. The New Testament joyfully proclaims to us, "Jesus is here!" What portrait is presented of Jesus in each of the following passages from the gospel of John?

Bible Verses	Portraits of Jesus
John 1:1–3, 14	
John 10:7–11	
John 11:25–26	
John 15:5–8	
John 19:16–19	
John 20:1–9	

3. According to the Bible passages below, what must we do to be made right with God?

   (Many phrases such as "to be made right with God," "to cross over from death to life," "to be saved," and "to become a Christian" all have the same meaning and are used to describe entering into a personal relationship with Jesus Christ.)

   John 5:24

   _____

   Romans 10:9–13

   _____

4. Write out the words of John 1:12. Then circle the action words in the verse.

   _____

   How do you think these action words sum up how we become a Christian?

   _____

   _____

5. Based on James 2:19, what kind of belief do you think God is looking for? (Is it a mental assent of the mind, or does He also desire a commitment of the heart?)

   _____

   _____

6. In Jesus' conversation with Nicodemus in John 3:1–7, how does Jesus describe becoming a Christian?

_____

_____

7. According to Revelation 3:20, where is Jesus right now?

_____

What is He doing right now?

_____

What is He waiting for you to do?

_____

What does He promise to do if you will do this?

_____

Do you want this for your own life?

_____

_____

_____

Illustration

A world-renowned tightrope walker arrived at Niagara Falls one day and immediately set up shop. As he placed his tightrope across the dangerous gap and prepared to make his first crossing, a crowd grew in number and in anticipation. Suddenly, they heard him call out, "Who believes that I can walk across these falls on this tightrope?" Most in the crowd were not sure, but a few urged him on, "We do, we do!" He proceeded to step onto the tightrope and walked across, much like you and I would cross a deserted small-town street.

He then turned to the crowd and asked, "Do you believe that I can cross these falls with a blindfold covering my eyes?" Several people gasped at the mere thought of such a proposition, but a growing number in the swelling crowd called out, "We believe you can!" Again, he made his way across the raging falls, this time unable to see where his next step might land. The ease of his achievement amazed everyone, for they had never seen such a sight.

A short time later, he appeared with a wheelbarrow and the question, "Do you believe that I can make the crossing pushing a wheelbarrow in front of me?" The surging crowd cheered him on, and again he did not disappoint them; he made the crossing with no difficulty.

Finally, he turned to the crowd and asked, "Do you believe that I can cross these falls pushing the wheelbarrow with somebody in it?" This time, the throngs of people knew better, and they answered, as with one voice, "We believe! We believe!" He paused for a moment. While appearing to scan and look at each one of them he asked, "Who will volunteer to sit in the wheelbarrow?"

The impact of his question slowly settled on each person and, one by one, they became silent. Most people, it seemed, had come to acknowledge that the tightrope walker could do what he claimed he would do. But no one was willing to trust him with his life.[10]

Food for Thought

"You can laugh at Christianity, you can mock and ridicule it. But it works. It changes lives. If you trust Christ, start watching your attitudes and actions, because Jesus Christ is in the business of changing lives."[11]

Josh McDowell

"He who provides for this life, but takes no care for eternity, is wise for a moment, but a fool forever."

John Tillotson

Memory Verse

"Yet to all who received him, to those who believed in his name, he gave the right to become children of God."—John 1:12

Mileposts

What are some of the things that God has taught you from your study of this chapter?

Moving On

Last chapter discussed Jesus' death that paid the penalty for sin. Salvation is a free gift from God, it can not be earned by our good works, and it is available to everyone through Jesus' sacrifice on the cross. However, we've learned that there must be a personal transaction between God and us.

You can receive God's free gift of salvation by trusting in Christ's death as payment for your sin and by receiving Him through personal invitation. When you do this, your sins are forgiven, your personal identity is made brand new, and your eternal destiny is forever changed. You also begin the greatest adventure this life offers, that of experiencing a personal, life-changing relationship with the living God who loves you more than you can ever know. While life does not suddenly become filled with ease and free of troubles, God promises to remain with you always.

Believing that Jesus died is a matter of history. But believing that Jesus died *for you* is a matter of salvation. Receiving salvation is as simple as receiving a free gift. Yet the paradox is that Jesus asks that you make a U-turn with your life, turning from your sins and, instead, living the way He has directed.

As our Creator, He loves us and is the Source of all wisdom and knowledge. He knows what is best for us and wants us to choose to follow His guidebook, the Bible. Since God is also the Creator and Source of all goodness, following His directives is for our good and benefit. He helps us do it, too, by sending His Spirit to live inside us and guide us. We give ourselves to Him—and He gives us Himself.

For those of us who are prone to doubt and disbelief, God provided ample proof that Jesus' claims are true. Jesus' earthly life fulfilled countless prophecies about the coming Savior that are recorded in the Old Testament. Jesus rose from the dead, leaving a long and glorious trail of evidence for His resurrection. He has transformed millions of lives throughout the centuries. And He wants to transform *yours*.

You can either receive Jesus' free gift of salvation, or you can reject it; you can either accept Jesus' payment of the penalty for your sins, or you can pay for them with your own death and eternal separation from God; you can stand before God either redeemed or condemned. The choice is yours to make. Are you willing to step into the wheelbarrow? Are you willing to trust Jesus with your very life? If you are, perhaps this prayer expresses your desire. There is no magic in the specific words, and you may certainly use your own. These words may help you express your desire to God:

Jesus, I thank You for loving me. I admit that I am a helpless sinner in need of a Savior. Thank You for being my Savior and for shedding Your blood on the cross in my place. Right now, I turn from my sin and I place my trust in You for my salvation. I trust Your death on the cross as payment for my sins, and I receive You right now into my life. I want to follow You and live for You. Thank You for coming into my life and for giving me eternal life. Amen.

If you've placed your trust in Jesus and prayed to receive Him into your life, then the Bible says that you are a new creation and that God has given you a brand-new life! The Bible also says that you can be assured of eternal life with God in heaven. To serve as a reminder of this important milepost, find somewhere on this page or in your Bible to make a note of the date or period of time when you made this decision. The next chapter will help you begin your adventure of growing as a follower of Jesus.

If, however, you have come to this point in your Bible study and, for one reason or another, have not chosen to trust Jesus for your salvation, there are several things that you should do. First, know that God will not take up residence in your life uninvited; He won't force His way on anyone, and He waits patiently for you to respond to His invitation. Second, if you have any questions or concerns, seek out a trusted Christian friend who can help you work through them and help you search the Bible for real answers. Third, do not wait too long—life does not guarantee you a tomorrow, and no other decision in your life will be more important or have more lasting impact than what you choose to do with Jesus Christ.

After Accepting Christ
LIVING IN RELATIONSHIP WITH GOD

If you prayed to receive Jesus and have placed your trust in Him for your salvation, the result is a spiritual transformation by the Holy Spirit, who is the Spirit of God, living inside you, guiding you into spiritual maturity. According to the Bible, you are a new creation.

In the physical realm, a newborn baby has his or her own unique identity and receives many privileges as a new family member. There are several important steps for that baby to grow to full maturity as a person. Similarly, in the spiritual realm, you, as a new baby in Christ, have a new identity, you have received many wonderful privileges as a child of God, and there are several ways that you can grow as a disciple of Jesus. This chapter can help start you on your journey with God.

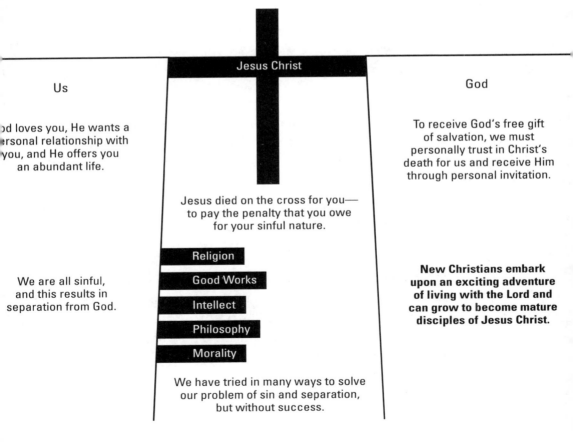

Jesus Christ

Us

God

od loves you, He wants a ersonal relationship with you, and He offers you an abundant life.

To receive God's free gift of salvation, we must personally trust in Christ's death for us and receive Him through personal invitation.

Jesus died on the cross for you— to pay the penalty that you owe for your sinful nature.

Religion

Good Works

Intellect

Philosophy

Morality

We are all sinful, and this results in separation from God.

New Christians embark upon an exciting adventure of living with the Lord and can grow to become mature disciples of Jesus Christ.

We have tried in many ways to solve our problem of sin and separation, but without success.

Up Close and Personal

TOM *and I were co-workers, and we frequently took walks together during lunch. As our friendship grew, our conversations centered on his struggles to be a good father and husband. As I shared with him the parenting and marriage wisdom of the Bible, he eventually decided that he wanted a relationship with the God of the Bible. More than ten years have now passed since Tom became a Christian, and his spiritual growth is a source of great joy. He recently led his oldest son, who's now experiencing similar parenting struggles, to the Lord. He has ministered through a Bible study at work, through a drama ministry at his church, and through his everyday life as a husband, father, and friend. Tom and I were recently reunited, and as we prayed together, the depth and closeness of his life with the Lord was quickly evident. God has beautifully transformed what was once a cold and hardened heart filled with anguish into a warm, softened heart of compassion.*

Reflecting back on my years before Christ, I feared the prospect of talking with other people about spiritual things, as Jay had done with me. I also found the Bible to be boring and difficult to understand. After beginning a relationship with Christ, many things changed (gradually, yet significantly) as I found ways to grow as a Christian. I planted myself within a college fellowship group, and the vibrance of my friends' faith was absolutely contagious. A hunger grew within me for the Word of God—to read, study, memorize, and obey it—and I now have a working understanding of it. My prayer life with God became more vibrant and intimate. And I found myself wanting to share the gospel message with my friends, not out of duty but out of a compelling passion. I left my bridge-engineering career to go to seminary. After graduating, however, I returned to engineering with the assurance that God can best use me as a layperson rather than as a pastor or missionary. Even with Christ, life is not always easy. But my worst days living with the Lord are better than my best days without Him. Life in Christ is abundant and adventurous and oh so good.

Getting Started

1. Write ten different answers to the question *Who am I?* in the space below. You may include roles and responsibilities, qualities and characteristics, relationships and commitments, beliefs and convictions. List whatever is really important to your sense of yourself. Then try to rank your answers in order of importance to you, with "1" being most important.

_____

_____

_____

_____

_____

_____

_____

_____

_____

_____

2. What are some of the greatest privileges you've been given?

_____

_____

3. In what specific ways have you changed since receiving Christ into your life?

_____

_____

Digging Deeper

1. When a person becomes a Christian, his or her identity is made new. Look up each of the verses below, and list in the middle column what is said about a Christian's identity. Then look at the table and circle the three descriptors that are the most meaningful to you, describing their significance in the right-hand column.

Bible Verses	The Christian's Identity	What does this mean to you?
Matthew 5:13–14		
Mark 1:17		
1 Corinthians 6:19–20		
1 Corinthians 12:27		
2 Corinthians 2:15		

Bible Verses	The Christian's Identity	What does this mean to you?
2 Corinthians 5:17		
2 Corinthians 5:20		
Ephesians 2:10		
1 Peter 2:9		
1 John 3:1		

2. As a member of God's family, you have been given many wonderful promises, assurances, and privileges. After looking up a verse in the first column, write the descriptor (listed above the table) in the middle column next to the corresponding verse. Then circle three privileges for which you are most grateful, and write in the right-hand column how they affect your life right now.

Answered prayer   God's inseparable love

Assurance of eternal life   God's presence

Forgiveness   Guidance

God's care   Holy Spirit

God's continual working   Victory over temptation

Bible Verses	The Christian's Privileges	How does this affect your life?
Proverbs 3:5–6		
John 16:24		
Romans 8:38–39		
1 Corinthians 10:13		
Ephesians 1:13–14		

Bible Verses	The Christian's Privileges	How does this affect your life?
Philippians 1:6		
Hebrews 13:5		
1 Peter 5:7		
1 John 1:9		
1 John 5:11–13		

3. There are many ways that you can grow to become a mature disciple of Jesus
   Christ. Look up each of the passages listed in the table below and on the following pages. In the left-hand column, jot down the phrase corresponding to it
   (see list of phrases above table). Then in the right-hand column, write what the
   verses teach you and how you can specifically apply them.

> A selfless, Christlike love for those God places around you
>
> A vibrant prayer life of conversing with God
>
> Building godly family relationships
>
> Discovering and using your spiritual gifts
>
> Living in the power of the Holy Spirit
>
> Making your life a witness for Christ in your world
>
> Obeying Jesus as Lord of your life
>
> Reading and studying God's Word regularly
>
> Remaining in community and fellowship with other Christians
>
> Worshiping God and giving Him praise and adoration

Ways to Grow as a Disciple of Jesus	What do you learn from these Bible passages and how can you apply them to life right now?
Bible Passages	
Joshua 1:8 *Psalm 119:9–16* *2 Timothy 2:15; 3:16*	
Philippians 4:6–7 *1 Thessalonians 5:16–18* *1 John 5:14–15*	

Ways to Grow as a Disciple of Jesus	What do you learn from these Bible passages and how can you apply them to life right now?
Bible Passages *Acts 2:42–47* *1 Corinthians 12:14–27* *Hebrews 10:24–25*	
     Mark 8:34–37 *John 14:15–21* *Romans 12:1–2*	
     Ephesians 5:21–6:4 *Colossians 3:18–21* *1 Peter 3:1–7*	
     Romans 12:3–8 *1 Corinthians 12:1–11* *Ephesians 4:11–13*	

Ways to Grow as a Disciple of Jesus	What do you learn from these Bible passages and how can you apply them to life right now?
Bible Passages *Matthew 28:18–20* *1 Thessalonians 2:4–8* *1 Peter 3:15–16*	
1 Chronicles 29:10–13 *Psalm 100* *Psalm 150*	
John 13:34–35 *1 Corinthians 13* *1 John 3:16–18; 4:7–21*	

Ways to Grow as a Disciple of Jesus	What do you learn from these Bible passages and how can you apply them to life right now?
Bible Passages	
John 16:7–15 *Acts 1:8* *Ephesians 5:18–20*	

What three listings in the right-hand column of the above table are the most important to you right now in your Christian life? Place a check mark (✓) next to them. Of those three, which one is most important to you right now? Place an asterisk (*) next to it.

Illustration

A new Christian embarked upon a long, adventurous journey. Preparing for the pilgrimage, the Christian came to Jesus and requested, "Lord, will You give me a road map showing me exactly where I'll be going? Which way am I to turn when I reach a fork in the road? How will I know if I'm going the right way? Where will I be five days from now? What about five years? And fifty years from now?"

A warm smile settled on Jesus' face as He replied, "I have no road map to offer you. But what I do offer you is Myself. If you'll let Me, I'll travel with you on your journey and guide you each step of the way. Besides, we'll enjoy being together and talking, and we can build quite a friendship throughout the journey."

Feeling reassured, they approached the car and the Christian then asked, "Will this old jalopy get us to our destination? How will I know what to do with it and how to take care of it?"

Jesus opened the glove compartment and pulled out a book. "Its creator developed an owner's manual for your use. It tells you all about the car."

"What if I don't follow it?" asked the Christian.

"You can choose to ignore the manual," Jesus replied, "and give your car a tune-up whenever you feel like it, and you are free to use diesel fuel in your engine instead of the intended unleaded gasoline if you wish. However, the result will be a considerably less pleasant journey. And we won't get very far. You can follow the creator's manual or ignore it. Certain inevitable consequences will follow."

Eager to begin the journey, the Christian excitedly climbed into the driver's seat. "Let's get started!" exclaimed the Christian. Noticing the empty seats in the car, Jesus said, "Wouldn't you like to bring others along on our journey? You could bring people who already know Me, and we could enjoy wonderful fellowship together. And you could invite people who don't know Me yet, and maybe if you introduce them to Me, they also would want to know Me and journey with us." The Christian readily agreed, and the seats in the old jalopy were filled with eager travelers in no time.

"One more thing before we go," Jesus told the Christian. "If I'm going to join you on your journey, I can't be in the passenger seat. You'll have to turn over the driver's seat to Me." So the Christian relinquished the driver's seat of the car to Jesus.

As they set out, the Christian questioned Jesus, "Aren't we going the wrong way?"

"Before we begin our journey," Jesus replied, "we need to go sign over the ownership of your car to Me."12

Food for Thought

"It is impossible for a believer, no matter what his experience, to keep right with God if he will not take the trouble to spend time with God.... Spend plenty of time with God; let other things go, but don't neglect Him."13

Oswald Chambers

"The world has yet to see what God will do with a person fully consecrated to the Lord Jesus Christ."14

spoken to D. L. Moody by Henry Varley

Memory Verse

"And this is the testimony: God has given us eternal life, and this life is in his Son. He who has the Son has life; he who does not have the Son of God does not have life. I write these things to you who believe in the name of the Son of God so that you may know that you have eternal life."—1 John 5:11–13

Mileposts

What are some of the things that God has taught you from your study of this chapter?

Moving On

We come to the end of our exploration of what God's Word says about beginning a personal relationship with our Creator. God loves you, He wants a personal relationship with you, and He offers you an abundant life. However, we are all sinful, and because of God's holiness and justice, our sinful nature separates us from God. Jesus died on the cross to pay the penalty that we owe for our sinful nature. Jesus did for us what religion, good works, intellect, philosophy, and morality are powerless to do. To receive God's free gift of salvation and become a Christian, we must personally trust in Christ's death for us and receive Him through personal invitation. As new Christians, we embark upon an exciting adventure of going on with God and growing to become mature disciples of Jesus.

We began our booklet with two important questions: "What do you think it means to be a Christian?" and "How would you respond if God were to ask you today, 'Why should I let you into My heaven?'" Some might say that a Christian is someone who goes to church and who is a good person. Others might respond that the way to heaven is following a religion or earning it by being good enough. Going to church, however, does not make anyone a Christian any more than being in a garage makes a mouse a car. And trying to earn heaven by your good life is a dead-end street, because you can never be good enough to meet God's perfect standard of holiness.

This chapter's study of the Bible has taught us that, when a person becomes a Christian, God makes him or her a new creation with a new identity. As new members of God's family, we are given many wonderful promises, assurances, and privileges, including God's forgiveness, His presence and care in our lives, and the Holy Spirit to reside within us and guide us. As new children of God, there are many ways that we can grow to become mature disciples of Jesus, including reading God's Word regularly, having a consistent prayer life, spending time interacting with other Christians, being a witness for Christ, and obeying Jesus as Lord.

As the traveler in our story learned, Jesus doesn't always provide us with the road map for all of our lives' journeys, but He gives us something far better. He promises to travel through life with us, guiding us at each turn and building a rich relationship with us at the same time. And just as the old jalopy came with an owner's manual, our Creator has supplied us with an owner's manual—the Bible. While we can choose to follow the Creator's manual or ignore it, we often do not have a choice about the consequences that result from our choices.

Just as Jesus did not want the traveler to leave with an empty car, He doesn't want us to travel through life alone either. Christians need each other, just as pieces of burning ember need each other to keep the fire aglow. And God has given us the wonderful privilege and responsibility of leading other people to Himself. Be sure to share the wonderful news in this booklet with someone else. And finally, just as Jesus insisted on the driver's seat in the jalopy, He wants the driver's seat of our lives as well, and He wants us to sign over our lives to Him.

Our memory verse for this chapter offers us the assurance of eternal life. Jesus' disciple John did not say, "I write these things to you who believe in the name of the Son of God so that you may *hope* that you have eternal life, or *wonder* if you'll have eternal life, or *think that you might* have eternal life." He said, "I write these things to you so that you may *know* that you have eternal life." God desires for you to know, with assurance, that when your earthly days are finished, your eternal destiny is with Him in heaven, enjoying His glorious presence and basking in His wondrous love.

Jesus does for us what religion can not do. Religion is spelled *do*. It is based on our attempts to try and be good enough to merit God's favor. Christianity is spelled *done*. It is based on what God has already accomplished through Christ's death, giving us His favor as a free gift because we could never be good enough to merit it.[15]

The founders of all the religions in the world have a grave somewhere where their bodies are buried. Jesus does not. He gloriously rose from the dead and is alive today, demonstrating the truth of His Word both in the power of His resurrection and in His continual activity in lives today.

The beautiful thing about being a Christian is that it is not so much following a religion as it is entering into a relationship—a loving relationship with the Creator of the universe!

We began our journey with God's love. We discovered that God loves us just as we are. And we end our journey with God's love—with the knowledge that He wants us to share a love relationship with Him and that He loves us too much to let us remain as we are.

The greatest privilege this life offers is to know the living God in a personal and vibrant way and to walk with Him through life's journey. Don't miss out on it!

Acknowledgments

This booklet is a product of countless people who have impacted my life and nurtured me as I have found God in the Bible and in my life.

To those who previewed this booklet or gave it a test run—Mike Addessi, Bill Amrhein, Frank Baker, Mark Bolton, Kate Chandler, Paul Cooper, Bill Daugherty, Greg Helsel, Chuck Horvath, Joe Leisinger, Jim Matyi, Wendy McFarland, Dave Meeks, Ann Rabovsky, Nancy Staible, Mom and Dad, and the participants in our "What is the Gospel Message?" Sunday school class— thanks for your valued wisdom and counsel, most of which made its way onto these pages. Special thanks to Pastors John Seth and Jeff Arnold, whose encouragement and support kept me going through many years of writing, testing, editing, and publishing.

To the gracious staff at Moody Publishers—especially Ali Childers, Elsa Mazon, Mark Tobey, and Amy Peterson—it is a delight working with each of you and a privilege being associated with Moody. I've experienced firsthand that Moody truly is a name you can trust.

To Mimi, Becca, and Andrew, thanks for your continual love and encouragement, which provide the greatest joys of my life.

To Jay Davis, thanks for your compassion and courage in gently leading me to the Savior (despite my stubbornness) and for changing my life forever.

Finally, and most importantly, I thank the Lord for His love and grace, without which the good news presented in this booklet would not exist and countless lives filled with peace and hope would instead be marked by emptiness and despair.

I write this booklet merely as one beggar longing to lead other beggars to the Source of abundant and eternal life.

Using this Booklet in a Small Group

Finding God in the Bible can be used within a small group of neighbors, co-workers, or family members. Here are a few suggestions for getting a small group started:

1. **Pray for opportunities to seek God with others.** Begin by praying that God will bring people into your life whom you can introduce to Him. This is a prayer that God delights to answer. He has created you and placed you right where you are for a reason. There are people who are curious about God all around you. You can find them in your neighborhood, workplace, family, school, or community. Invite them to seek God with you.

2. **Earn trust over time.** Spend time with people who want to find

out more about God, building genuine friendships with them. After all, people aren't projects; people are unique creations of God with different experiences at different points in life. Our love for others should not be based upon their responses to spiritual things.

3. **Be open.** After you choose the time and place for a first small group meeting, invite people! Be sure you are creating an environment where people feel safe sharing and discussing their fears and concerns. Be open to conversation, but also be ready to back off and give people space. It takes time to build intimate friendships. Additionally, sometimes people just don't click. Don't take it personally if the group isn't right for someone and they don't want to keep coming.

After you've laid the groundwork, you're ready to start the small group. *Finding God in the Bible* is designed to provide the content. Here are some suggestions for how to lead a small group:

1. **Take individual spiritual journeys into consideration.** Since people are at different places in their spiritual lives, the group should commit to listening to one another and sharing beliefs and ideas with respect and without hostility. No one should feel rejected through the conversations. Try not to put anyone on the spot by asking them to read or pray out loud—instead, ask for a volunteer. This study is designed to start with the basics and build upon them.

2. **Use icebreakers.** Ask one or two ice-breaker questions every time you meet. Ice-breaker questions are designed to open up the group and to allow them to see that they all share similar needs and struggles, hopes, and fears. The "Getting Started" section of each chapter provides several examples, and you can also craft your own ice-breakers.

3. **Ask thought-provoking questions.** Seek to master the skill of asking questions that can guide the conversation to a deeper level. Allow the group to self-discover spiritual truths. Give them center stage; you become part of the listening audience. Do more asking than telling.

4. **Don't get discouraged or be discouraging.** It's okay if you're not a Bible scholar. The best leaders are often those who *don't* have all the answers. Don't give two-cent answers to million-dollar questions—in other words, don't oversimplify a difficult question with a trite, simple answer.

5. **Don't be a lone ranger.** Surround yourself with a few other Christians to join you. Find some people who love people, and just let them do it. One person could host the group at their home, another could assist leading the group. Let others talk about their spiritual pilgrimages.

6. **All people are important.** Honor others as they are in the process of discovering more about God. Everyone ought to feel important. Remember that all people matter to God, and they should matter to us also.[16]

Using this Booklet with a Friend

Finding God in the Bible can also be used one-on-one with a friend. Here are some suggestions:

1. **Be a friend.** Continue building your friendship, regardless of the other person's response to spiritual things. Loving friendships are not based upon one person's ability to change the other. Be eager to listen. Don't wear out your friend by talking about yourself all the time. If you are talking more than half of the time, then you are talking too much.

2. **Allow God to work.** The gospel is not a message that is to be used like a club with which to threaten or beat another person. As 1 Peter 3:15 says, "Always be prepared to give an answer to everyone

who asks you to give the reason for the hope that you have. But do this with gentleness and respect." Ask the Holy Spirit to work in your hearts and for God to guide you into the truth about Himself.

3. **Ask open-ended questions.** There is often greater power in a well-crafted question than in giving another person "answers" they weren't asking to receive. Questions facilitate self-discovery. They also keep either one of you from dominating the conversation or "preaching" at each other. Don't be a know-it-all; share in the discovery process.

4. **Be real and be vulnerable.** When you spend time together, allow your friend to see the real you. People can see right through phoniness. Share your struggles as well as your joys, your defeats as well as your victories. By being honest and genuine, you will enable your friend to also be honest with you as well.

5. **Accept each other.** Don't condemn your friend for failing or sinning. While God hates our sin, He passionately loves us sinners. We should do the same in relation to each other. You are both in need of God's help, grace, and mercy.

6. **Stick with the main issue.** Although tangents will inevitably break off from your conversations, don't allow them to dominate your times together. The issue at hand is people's need for a personal relationship with Jesus Christ to make them right with God. Don't allow yourselves to stray too far from this.

7. **Call each other to action.** The gospel message inherently calls for a personal decision. Each person needs to decide if they are for or against a personal relationship with Jesus Christ. Don't be afraid to draw each other out and talk about this decision. God wants to use us to help one another come closer to Him, which is why He calls us to be fishers of people (Mark 1:17).

8. **Have fun together.** Look for common interests and do things together! Go to a game together, throw a party, go on a double date,
   share a weekly meal. You might just find that some great conversations and insights come during your casual times together.[17,18]

Glossary of Common Bible Terms

Atone—to pay or make up for a wrong act; Jesus Christ atoned for our sins when He died on the cross

Baptism—shows that we are members of God's family and symbolizes our sins being buried in Christ's death and us being raised to eternal life, our sins washed away

Believe—to have faith or to trust; Christian belief includes a concurrance that the Bible is truth and trusting in Jesus as Savior

Born again—to receive God's free gift of salvation, making one spiritually reborn

Christ—God's Chosen One, the Messiah; the One sent by the Father to restore us to Himself

Christian—one who believes that Jesus is God's Son and trusts Him for salvation from sin; a follower of Christ

Church—the local gathering of Christians, or all Christians everywhere; the people of God

Condemn—to declare guilty of doing something wrong and to assign a just punishment

Confess—to admit your sins to God; to acknowledge your faith to others

Death—the end of life; the Bible speaks of both physical death and spiritual death

Disciple—a student or follower of someone; one who trusts Jesus as Lord and Master and obeys Him

Faith—to trust someone because of who they are; to be certain about things we can not yet see

Fear of the Lord—respect and reverential awe for God because of His perfection, sovereignty, and holiness

Forgive—to pardon or acquit of sins; to not retaliate and hurt someone who has hurt you

Gospel—the message that Jesus died for our sins and offers us new life; literally "good news"

Grace—God's favor toward us though we don't deserve it; "God's riches at Christ's expense"

Heaven—the home of God, the angels, and those granted salvation; the place where those who trust Christ for salvation will live forever with Jesus

Hell—the place of torment and separation from God where the spiritually lost will spend eternity

Holy—pure and perfect, without sin; set apart and belonging to God

Holy Spirit—the personal, but unseen, power and presence of God in the Christian's life and in the world

Justified—to be declared right with God through faith in Christ

Law—the rules God gave us to help us know and love Him and live peacefully with each other

Lord—Master; the One whom we obey and to whom we submit our lives

Lost—strayed or misplaced; one who is not trusting in Christ for their salvation; condemned

Made right(eous)—to be put into a restored relationship with God; to receive salvation through Jesus Christ

Mediator—one who comes between parties in conflict with each other and settles differences; Jesus became our mediator by taking our sins that separate us from God and giving us His righteousness

Propitiation—the sacrifice of Christ, which turns aside God's anger and wrath toward us

Receive—to take possession of that which is not earned; to believe or accept as true; to welcome Jesus as Savior

Reconcile—to restore or reunite those who have been separated; Jesus reconciles us to God

Redeem—to buy back; by dying for us, Jesus paid the price to "buy us back" to God and free us from sin

Repent—to turn around; to change your heart and your behavior; a moral U-turn from sin

Righteous—living a right and holy life; God sees Christians as righteous because of Christ's sinless record now given to them

Saint—God's people; the Bible says that all Christians are saints

Salvation—deliverance from sin; God's rescue of those who trust in Jesus' death on the cross as payment for their sin

Sanctified—set apart for God's use; purified and cleansed; to become more and more like Jesus

Saved—our being rescued from the eternal consequences of our sin

Savior—the One who saves us from our sin; Jesus Christ

Sin—to miss the mark; to fall short of the way God wants us to live; all have sinned, and sin separates us from God

Soul—the essence of our life and being; our control center; that part of us which is eternal

Trust—to place our confidence in; we can trust Christ to make us right with God

Wages—the fair payment; the Bible says that the wages of our sin is spiritual death

Walk—the manner in which we live; Christians can walk with God each day, being "in step" with His Spirit

Witness—to tell what one has seen or heard; to testify to the truth

Word of God—words spoken by God; the Bible

Works—actions and deeds; good works can not save us, but they are the response to our salvation

Worship—to show love and respect for that which you value most; God is worthy of our worship and praise[19]

Notes

1. Adapted from The Navigators, *Bridge to Life* (Colorado Springs: NavPress, 1969). For more information about this tract, call 800-366-7788 or see www.navpress.com.

2. Donald Grey Barnhouse, *Let Me Illustrate* (Westwood, N.J.: Fleming H. Revell, 1967), 215.

3. Augustine, *Confessions* (AD 400).

4. Adapted from Steven Curtis Chapman and Geoff Moore, "Treasure of You," *Heaven in the Real World,* compact disc, Sparrow Song, 1994.

5. Adapted from a talk by Bill Hybels, Indianapolis, June 3, 1994.

6. Ibid.

7. Adapted from a talk by Bill Collier, Harmony-Zelienople United Methodist Church, Zelienople, Pa., 1990, and adapted from Paul E. Little, *How to Give Away Your Faith* (Downers Grove, Ill.: InterVarsity Christian Fellowship, 1966).

8. Billy Graham, *Peace with God* (Nashville: W Publishing, 1953, 1984).

9. James S. Hewett, *Illustrations Unlimited* (Wheaton, Ill.: Tyndale, 1988), 38.

10. Adapted from talks by Gary Bradley, Ithaca, N.Y., 1978 and Adin Herndon, Carlisle, Pa., 1981.

11. Josh McDowell, *More Than a Carpenter* (Wheaton, Ill.: Tyndale, 1977), 128.

12. Adapted from a talk by Bob Vidano, "The Gap," Ocean City, Md., 1980.

13. Oswald Chambers, *My Utmost for His Highest: An Updated Edition in Today's Language*, trans. James Reimann (Grand Rapids: Discovery House, 1992).

14. Spoken to D. L. Moody by evangelist Henry Varley. Moody resolved to be that person.

15. Adapted from Mark Mittelberg, Lee Strobel, and Bill Hybels, *Becoming a Contagious Christian: Participant's Guide* (Grand Rapids: Zondervan, 1995), 64.

16. Adapted from Garry Poole, *Seeker Small Groups* (Grand Rapids: Zondervan, 2003).

17. Adapted from Paul E. Little, *How to Give Away Your Faith* (Downers Grove, Ill.: InterVarsity Christian Fellowship, 1966).

18. Adapted from John Fischer, "The Friendship Account," *DECISION* (January 1998): 16–18.

19. Adapted from Henrietta C. Mears, *What the Bible Is All About* (Ventura, Calif.: Regal Books, 1997).

Additional Resources

To Help You Understand the Gospel Message

1. Billy Graham, *Steps to Peace With God* (Minneapolis: Billy Graham Evangelistic Association, 1954).

   This 16-page booklet presents the basic gospel message in a clear and concise manner. Filled with Bible verses and simple illustrations, it is ideally suited to help anyone better understand the basic message of salvation. See http://www.billygraham.org for ordering information.

2. Bill Bright, *Have You Heard of the Four Spiritual Laws?* (San Bernardino, Calif.: Campus Crusade for Christ, 1965).

   Similar to *Steps to Peace With God,* this small booklet includes valuable follow-up information for new believers, including suggestions for Christian growth. Over one billion copies of this 16-page booklet are in print.

3. C. S. Lewis, *Mere Christianity* (New York: Macmillan, 1943).

   Written by a professor of medieval and renaissance literature at Cambridge University, and arguably the most original Christian writer of the twentieth century, this timeless book will challenge your intellect and satisfy your desire to blend the beliefs of your heart and mind.

4. Josh McDowell, *More Than a Carpenter* (Wheaton, Ill.: Tyndale, 1977).

   Josh McDowell's book focuses on the person who changed his life, Jesus Christ. Like its companion, *Evidence That Demands a Verdict,* this is a hard-hitting book for people who are skeptical about Jesus' deity, His resurrection, and His claims on their lives.

5. John Stott, *Basic Christianity* (Downers Grove, Ill.: InterVarsity Press, 1958).

   This distinguished Anglican pastor from London provides a sound and sensible guide for those who are seeking a highly intellectually satisfying presentation of the Christian faith.

6. The Navigators, *Bridge to Life* (Colorado Springs: NavPress, 1969).

   Like the two booklets mentioned above, this 16-page booklet presents the basic message of salvation and includes Bible verses and illustrations.

To Help You Grow As a New Christian

1. Oswald Chambers, *My Utmost for His Highest: An Updated Edition in Today's Language,* trans. James Reimann (Grand Rapids: Discovery House, 1992).

   This devotional book of daily readings for the year has challenged countless Christians to a life of discipline, godliness, prayer, and spiritual growth; it continues to be a perennial bestseller.

2. Robert A. Cook, *Now That I Believe* (Chicago: Moody, 1986).

    Dealing with the basics of the Christian life, this simple, informal book offers counsel from both biblical text and human experience.

3. Paul E. Little, *Know What You Believe* (Wheaton, Ill.: Victor Books, 1970).

    Like its companion, *Know Why You Believe,* this book has helped countless new and longtime Christians better understand the basic truths of their faith.

4. Robert Boyd Munger, *My Heart—Christ's Home* (Downers Grove, Ill.: InterVarsity Press, 1954).

    Imagine what it would be like to have Christ come to the home of your heart. This classic story takes us room by room as we consider with our Lord what He desires for our lives.

5. Charles M. Sheldon, *In His Steps* (Nashville: Thomas Nelson, 1999).

    This novel, written in 1897, is a timeless classic, illustrating what happens when Christians in a local church pledge to not do anything without first asking the question, "What would Jesus do?" and then follow in Christ's steps regardless of what others might think.

6. The Navigators, *Design for Discipleship* (Colorado Springs: NavPress, 1973).

    This seven-volume set of Bible study books is designed to help you establish a program of personal study of God's Word, examine the great truths of the Bible, and learn and practice the essentials of discipleship.

SINCE 1894, Moody Publishers has been dedicated to equip and motivate people to advance the cause of Christ by publishing evangelical Christian literature and other media for all ages, around the world. Because we are a ministry of the Moody Bible Institute of Chicago, a portion of the proceeds from the sale of this book go to train the next generation of Christian leaders.

If we may serve you in any way in your spiritual journey toward understanding Christ and the Christian life, please contact us at www.moodypublishers.com.

"All Scripture is God-breathed and is useful for teaching, rebuking, correcting and training in righteousness, so that the man of God may be thoroughly equipped for every good work."
—2 TIMOTHY 3:16, 17

MOODY
PUBLISHERS

THE NAME YOU CAN TRUST®

FINDING GOD IN THE BIBLE TEAM

ACQUIRING EDITOR
Mark Tobey

COPY EDITOR
Ali Childers

BACK COVER COPY
Elizabeth Cody Newenhuyse

COVER DESIGN
BlueFrog Design

INTERIOR DESIGN
BlueFrog Design

PRINTING AND BINDING
Color House Graphics

The typeface for the text of this book is
AGaramond